EYE OF THE STORM:

Where is God when life hurts?

Alexander Kumpf

WESTBOW
PRESS
A DIVISION OF THOMAS NELSON

Chapter 5 "The Farmer" www.sermonillustration.com © 2011

Chapter 9 "Shipwreck" Green Michael P 1500 Illustrations for Biblical Preaching. Baker Books © 1982, 1985, 1989

Unless otherwise indicated, Scripture taken from the Holy Bible, New International Version®. Copyright © 1973, 1978, 1984 Biblica. Used by permission of Zondervan. All rights reserved.

All other Scripture quotations in this publications are from The Message. Copyright (c) by Eugene H. Peterson 1993, 1994, 1995, 1996, 2000, 2001, 2002. Used by permission of NavPress Publishing Group.

Scripture taken from the Amplified Bible, Copyright © 1954, 1958, 1962, 1964, 1965, 1987 by The Lockman Foundation. Used by permission.

Jacket Design: Kegan Schott

WestBow Press books may be ordered through booksellers or by contacting:
WestBow Press
A Division of Thomas Nelson
1663 Liberty Drive
Bloomington, IN 47403
www.westbowpress.com
1-(866) 928-1240

Because of the dynamic nature of the Internet, any web addresses or links contained in this book may have changed since publication and may no longer be valid. The views expressed in this work are solely those of the author and do not necessarily reflect the views of the publisher, and the publisher hereby disclaims any responsibility for them.

Any people depicted in stock imagery provided by Thinkstock are models, and such images are being used for illustrative purposes only.
Certain stock imagery © Thinkstock.

ISBN: 978-1-4497-3089-5 (sc)
ISBN: 978-1-4497-3090-1 (hc)
ISBN: 978-1-4497-3088-8 (e)

Library of Congress Control Number: 2011960129

Printed in the United States of America

WestBow Press rev. date: 11/18/2011

Contents

Introduction

Wouldn't it be great if life was like a weather report? Today's weather is cloudy with a 30 percent chance of anxiety and a slight depression. A cold front will be coming in earlier next week and will merge with an economic recession. By next Friday, things will look better as arguments with your spouse begin to clear up.

We would love to know which of life's storms are approaching before they actually get here so we could just get out of the way and let them pass. However, this is not the case. Storms of life come suddenly and unexpectedly. We live in an unpredictable world. Sometimes life can become very hard for us, and its storms will not let up. During these times, we feel hurt, worried, hopeless, and confused. However, there is hope! There is hope because there is God.

Unfortunately, too many people blame God for their misfortune, which just makes their situation worse. Instead of trusting and relying on God during their time of need, they point their finger at God and accuse Him of some divine criminal act against humanity. God knows what storms are brewing out there, and He knows how to get us through. We just need to learn to trust His guidance as he steers our ship through the treacherous waters so we can safely get to shore. I am hoping that we will come to understand that God is not necessarily the cause of life's chaotic mess, but he is the answer to overcoming any storm we encounter in life.

God, I pray for all those who read the words of this book to remember that these are your words. I ask that you give them strength and power to overcome any challenging situation in their lives. Let them come to understand that you are the one who comforts us in our time of need, and that you are a safe place to run and hide when we begin to feel the intensity of life's bitter winds and rain. You are the light that shatters the darkness, and your glory breaks forth through the dark clouds, reminding us that there are always better days ahead. In Jesus' name. Amen.

1

Storms Will Come

————◆————

LIFE IS NOT EASY

Whoever says "Life is easy" must be living on a different planet because life on this planet is not easy. It is hard. We regularly face misfortune, misery, and distress. As the storms of life continually leave us in chaotic cataclysms, we began to struggle within ourselves: How do I cope when I lose a love one, endure a painful argument, face a crushing financial situation, or handle painful disappointments? How do I even start to fathom a world full of evil, injustice, and pain?

What about the times when we feel the sullen rains of family arguments, brace for the winds of economic change, or face the bitter coldness of loneliness, anxiety, and depression? What happens when the weather changes, and we watch the dark clouds roll in as the doctor says, "I am sorry, but the results came back and you have cancer?" These are the moments that put us to the test. We start asking, "Why is this happening? What did I do to deserve this? Is there any hope? Where is God?"

CAMPING TRIP

I remember back in high school, three of my friends, Dan, Jim, Chris, and I wanted to go camping for the weekend. So one Friday afternoon, we packed up our gear, loaded the truck, and headed for the Econfina River in North Florida. We drove about an hour and half to the river, parked the truck, unloaded, rented our canoes, and paddled another mile down the river to our camping spot. We finally reached our destination, unpacked, and set up camp. That night, we slept well and awoke early to all-day activities of swimming, canoeing, and fishing. It was just one of those times in life when all was right with the world; when you could possibly say, "How can anything go wrong?"

That night, as I was sleeping peacefully in my sleeping bag, I was rudely awakened at three a.m. by Dan poking me in the head with his finger. "Alex! Wake up! We have to go, man!"

Startled, I woke up immediately. I could hear the pounding of rain, the booming of thunder, and could barely make out images in the tent by the flashes of lightning. As my eyes adapted to the dimness, I noticed the rest of my friends scrambling along, trying to pick up all their stuff. As I looked down, I was horrified by what I saw. The tent was quickly filling up with water! We all jumped out of the tent with our gear, tore down the tent, and started throwing everything in the canoes. Well, actually, Dan and I threw everything into Jim and Chris's canoe.

We pushed our canoes into the water and took off upstream toward the truck. The freezing rain was torrential, and we were tired. The only time we could see the river, trees, or anything was when the lightning flashed. My muscles ached as we tried to steer the canoe from side to side, dodging every tree limb, rock, and log in the fast-flowing stream. I thought for a moment, *This isn't too bad we can make it. We are going to make it through this storm.*

Just as my pride was rising up within me, I felt a sudden pull under the canoe. I heard a scrape, and then I realized what happened. Our canoe was caught on a log. We were stuck. I looked up just as Jim and Chris's canoe vanished behind the bend. So, there we were, Dan and I, stuck in the middle of our storm in the torrential rain with no one to help us. We looked at each other, panicked. Dan asked, "Alex, how can we get out of this?"

I answered, "You can get out and push."

Dan didn't think that was very funny. We decided to rock the canoe and then push it off the log with our paddle, hoping that would free us. We were not successful. Finally, we just cried out to God for help. We knew He could set us free! At that moment, the water seemed to shift, and we decided to try one more shove. We put both are paddles on the log, pushed with all our might, and finally the log let us go from its clutches. We were free!

We spent another thirty minutes paddling upstream to our destination. When we got there, Jim and Chris had already packed the truck and were waiting for us with the heater running. We left our canoe on the bank, climbed in the cab of the truck, and drove home.

This story is a reminder that at any moment in life we can be rudely awakened by the torrential winds and rains of life. Storms come in a variety of ways. We do not all face the same storms, but no matter how small or large, strong or fierce, they will eventually show up in our lives. If we are really going to learn how to trust God and overcome the storms in our lives, we must first understand this simple truth: Storms *will* come!

JESUS TOLD US THEY WOULD COME

Even Jesus did not hide the fact that life will bring painful situations. He said, "In this godless world, you will continue to experience difficulties" (John 16:33 NIV). He never said, "You might have trouble," or "As a Christian, every day is going to be perfect." He plainly says, "You *will* have trouble, you *will* continue to experience difficulties." Denial is not going to make them go away. You cannot hide from them. You cannot avoid them. You cannot not just stick your head in the sand and pretend that the storms don't exist.

JESUS HELPS US OVERCOME

The only way to survive a storm is to face it head-on. Jesus continued, saying, "But be of good cheer [take courage; be confident; certain, undaunted] for I have overcome the world [I have deprived it of power to harm you and have conquered it for you]" (John 16:33b AMP). Did you catch that? Jesus has deprived the storm's power to harm you. That means that even though a storm creeps into your life, it has no control over you. It cannot take away your joy. It cannot take away your faith. It cannot steal your purpose. It has no ability to separate you from God's love, and you have the power to decide how the storm is going to affect you. The storm will only take from you what you decide to give it.

Remember, Jesus said, "Be of good cheer," or, in other words, have courage! Be fearless! Jesus is the winner, and in him, you are already on the winning team. Why? Because the One who already won the victory won't abandon you when you feel defeat. He is like the quarterback of the big game leading us to the winning touchdown! You just need to follow his plays for your life.

When we continually put our trust in him, no matter what happens, the end result will always be a win, a victory! We have supernatural power from Jesus to overcome every problem, trial, hurt, and pain that comes our way. Paul tells us, "The Spirit of God, who raised Jesus from the dead, lives in you" (Romans 8:11a). The same power that brought Jesus back to life is alive in you! This means that through the Holy Spirit you have the same ability as Jesus to overcome every obstacle that life throws at you—even *death* is not the end.

GOD REMAINS FAITHFUL

During the storm, it is sometimes impossible to understand how God will pull us through, but he always does! He is faithful! The Bible promises us that God will remain faithful to us even when life becomes confusing and difficult. Psalm 57:10 says,

"The faithfulness of God reaches to the sky ..." That means that it is unlimited! It is unending! It cannot be measured! It will never run out! Psalm 117:2 extends this principle: "The faithfulness of the Lord endures forever ..." God will never give up on you. He will continue to fulfill his promises for you, in you, and to you. The prophet Isaiah reminds us that God will not quit on us in our time of need. "I will turn the darkness into light before them and make the rough places smooth. These are the things I will do; I will not forsake them" (Isaiah 42:16b).

Do you feel like the weather is changing? Do you feel the wind picking up? Do you see the dark clouds moving in, blocking the warmth of the sun? Then go find shelter in the faithfulness of God. God's task is to bring you through the storm; your task is to trust him during the storm.

2

Where Is God?

———⊰◆⊱———

9/11

I will never forget where I was on the morning of
September 11, 2001. I was attending Southeastern
University in Lakeland, Florida, living in an
apartment off campus. I forgot to set my alarm
the night before and was awakened by my cell
phone ringing. When I answered, I heard my
friend yelling, "Turn on the TV! Turn on the TV!
You are not going to believe this! Buildings in New
York were hit! I ... I have to go." *Click.*

Very confused, I put down the phone, picked
up the remote, and turned on the TV. And then I
saw images of the towers burning. I knew at that

moment this was going to be a day that would change America forever. As the day continued, I noticed that people kept asking two questions: Who did this? Where was God?

We soon discovered the answer to the first question: Terrorists from the Mideast planned and executed an attack on the United States. However, the second question kept burning in the hearts and minds of Americans. The next weekend, church attendance skyrocketed across the country. People all over America went to houses of worship to find an answer to this question, "Where was God?"

IS GOD SLEEPING ON THE JOB?

So where is God in the midst of storms and tragedy? Is he sleeping on the job? Taking a vacation? Does he even care anymore? We are not alone in asking these questions—even the disciples asked similar questions when they were trapped in the middle of a violent windstorm. In Mark 4, Jesus, having just finished a two-day healing conference, tells his disciples, "Let's go across to the other side [of the lake]." As they took him in the boat, other boats came along. A huge storm came up. Waves poured into the boat, threatening to sink it. And Jesus was in the stern, sleeping! They roused him, saying, "Teacher, is it nothing to you that we're going down?" Awake now, he told the wind to pipe down and said to the sea, "Quiet! Settle down!" The wind ran out of breath; the sea became smooth as glass. Jesus reprimanded the disciples, "Why are you such cowards? Don't you have any faith at all?" They were in absolute awe, staggered. "Who is this any way?" they asked. "Wind and sea are his beck and call" (Mark 4:35–41 MSG).

DON'T KICK JESUS OUT

First, Jesus says, "Let us go." God goes with us on the journey. He doesn't leave us to fend for ourselves. He is right there every step of the way; helping us, guiding us, and leading us. God assures us, "I'll never let you down, never walk off and leave you."(Hebrews 13:5b MSG).

Unfortunately, some people do not want God to go with them. They end up pushing him out of the boat, and when storms arise, they look for him but cannot find him. They have no captain steering the ship through the treacherous waters. They have no navigator to guide them through life's most difficult times. God wants to help them, but they keep telling God, "I don't want your help! I don't need your help!" What they are really saying is, "God, I don't need you! I don't want you!" When God reaches out, they push his hand away. When God steps forward, they take two steps back. When God tries to talk, they walk away. God really takes this seriously. He gives a stern warning about this in Proverbs 1:23–28:

> Look, I'm ready to pour out my spirit on you; I'm ready to tell you all I know. As it is, I've called, but you've turned a deaf ear; I've reached out to you, but you've ignored me. Since you laughed at my counsel and make a joke of my advice, how can I take you seriously? I'll turn the tables and joke about your troubles! What if the roof falls in, and your whole life goes to pieces? What if catastrophe strikes and there's nothing to show for your life but rubble and ashes? You'll need me then. You'll call for me, but don't expect an answer. No matter how hard you look, you won't find me.

These may sound like harsh words, but they are also honest words. When people want to weather the storm by themselves, pride swells up inside of them, and they tell themselves, "I don't need any help! I can do it on my own! No one is going to tell me what to do, especially some god!" God then lets them have their way. Proverbs 16:18 reminds us, "Pride leads to destruction, and arrogance to downfall.". God will not force himself on anyone. If we kick God out, he will leave us alone.

So how do we invite God back? Simple. We invite him back with a humble spirit. God responds better to humility than to hollow, empty, distant, and arrogant cries of help. The Bible explains, "God opposes the proud but gives grace to the humble ... Humble yourselves, therefore, under God's mighty hand, that he may lift you up in due time" (1 Peter 5:6). Is God willing and ready to help? Yes, he is, but only to those who are humble in spirit. Those who realize they can't do it on their own. Those who say, "God, I am sorry I rejected you, but I know you can do all things. I am really scared and confused. Can you help me? I will trust you no matter what because I believe your way is better." So to me the question isn't whether God is willing to help. The real question is, "Am I willing to humbly trust God?"

JESUS WILL GET US THROUGH

The disciples were willing to trust Jesus and took him in the boat. Jesus was with them before the storm even happened, and he gives this promise, "We are going to the other side." Jesus doesn't say, "I think we can cross this lake. I don't really know if we will make it, but it's worth a shot." No, he says, "We *are* going to the other side."

God knows the destination. He has the plan. He's weathered the storm before. He knows exactly how to get us through. It's as if Jesus is saying, "You might not know what storm lies ahead of you, but I know the storm, and it's not as scary as it looks. I am not intimidated by the weather, but the weather is intimidated by me. If you only trust my leading, I will make sure you get to the other side. If you follow my directions, I will not let you be lost at sea." When we start to understand God's devotion to us, we begin to develop a sense of courage rising within us. Hebrews tells us, "We can boldly quote, 'God is there, ready to help; I'm fearless no matter what. Who or what can get to me? (Hebrews 13:6–8 MSG).

GOD IS BIGGER

Yes, life's problems can be threatening, overwhelming, and ferocious, but no matter how strong a storm gets, God will always be stronger, and no matter how big a storm becomes, God is always bigger! The disciples needed to realize how much bigger their God was when a huge storm came out of nowhere. The Amplified Bible says that the storm had "hurricane proportions" (Mark 4:37). This must have been some wild tempest since it scared the disciples. Four of the disciples, Andrew, James, John, and Peter, were commercial fishermen. They must have worked and made their living on this lake. Surely they battled such storms during their lifetimes? However, this time they were scared, confused, and went into panic mode. So they looked around for the one person who could rescue them from such a frightening dilemma and found him sleeping on the job. This led them to wonder, "Don't you care about the raging storm we are encountering?" as we wonder, "God, don't you care about what I am going through?"

However, look at Jesus' response. The Bible says he just got up and spoke three little words, "Quiet, be still!" (Mark 4:39 NIV). Jesus did not run away from the problem; he conquered it. With three words, he changed the entire outcome of the situation. Where there was chaos, there was now peace; where there was torment, there was now comfort; where there was despair, there was now hope. The disciples' questions quickly turned from, "Do you care?" to "Who is this?" From saying, "We are going to drown," to "the wind and waves obey him."

What if they had not gone through this storm? What if the storm wasn't as fierce? What if they didn't experience fear during the storm? Would they have ever witnessed Jesus' power to bring peace during times of crisis?

AN UNEXPECTED VISITOR

In 1979, my mother was diagnosed with a brain tumor. She was married, with two kids. I was only one, and my sister was six. The doctors didn't know what they could do, and it looked really hopeless from a medical viewpoint. Back then, people just didn't know much about brain tumors, let alone how to cure them. My mom's life was literally hanging in the balance. The storm was raging. She watched the dark clouds taking away her hope, felt the harsh rains flooding her mind with fear, and sensed the strong winds of doubt eroding her faith. Day after day, week after week, month after month, she prayed, hoping that God would give her an answer. She was mad, mad at life, mad at the situation, and mad at God.

Then one afternoon, in tears of frustration, she cried out to God, "Why are you doing this? What did I do to deserve this? Do you even care? What about my family? Please, God, please help me!"

At that exact moment, she heard a knock at the door. She slowly got up, wiped her eyes, composed herself, and went to answer the door. Opening it, she was surprised to see a clean-shaven young man. He was nicely dressed with a button-down shirt. His hair was brown, medium length, and combed back. Perplexed, my mom said in a very shaky voice, "Hello. How can I help you?"

The gentleman gave a small sigh and replied, "Hello, ma'am. You do not know me, and we have never met before. My name is Bruce. I do not want to startle you, but God spoke to me concerning you."

My mom wondered, *Is the guy for real? Who is this wacko, standing on my front porch?* She politely told the gentleman that she was busy, but thanked him for coming.

However, the unexpected visitor insisted, "Please, ma'am. This is very important for you. Just give me a few minutes." My mom decided to listen to him. With sincerity in his voice, he continued, "As I was driving down the main highway, I heard God speak to me. He told me, 'Make the next right.' So I did. I then felt him direct me to take the next left, pass the second house on the right, make another left, and turn down this street. As I came upon your house, I felt a strong pull inside of me to park in front of this house, get out, and knock on your door. As I was getting out of my van, I heard these words in my heart, 'The woman who lives in this house is dealing with a painful struggle. She doesn't understand what is happening to her, but I will show her my power." Bruce then looked directly in to my mother's eyes, and with much love and compassion, said, "Ma'am, God wants me to tell you that everything is going to be all right. If you trust God, He will make everything all right."

My mom just stood there in shock. She couldn't move, couldn't say a word. She just stared at him, with wide-open eyes.

Finally Bruce said, "Ma'am, I hope you have a pleasant day, and may God bless you." He walked away, got into his van, drove off, and disappeared around the corner.

As my mom slowly closed the door, the storm that was raging in her heart began to calm. Fear turned to hope, doubt turned to faith, and confused thoughts turned to a peace of mind. Eventually, God led her to the right neurosurgeon, and a few months later, she had the surgery and was completely healed. My mom lives today, with no signs of any tumor. God came through in the midst of her storm. She learned an important lesson that day: Even in our darkest times when we can't see God working, God is still working.

GOD IS ALWAYS WORKING

God is always up to something, and that something is always good. Paul tells us in Romans 8:28, "For we know that in all things God works for the good of those who love him, who have been called according to his purposes." That verse became reality to my mother. It was no longer just a nice, polite thing you say to someone in time of need when you don't know what else to say. Paul's words have a deeper, more dynamic meaning. God works. His works are powerful, his works are good, and his works are life changing. God is able to take any situation in our lives, no matter how grueling, harsh, and painful, and turn it into something good, exceptional, and wonderful.

So where is God during storms? He's right there, ready to help navigate you through the wind and the waves. Many times, God takes us right through the heart of the storm so we can eventually see His life-changing power working within us. As long as Jesus is in the stern of your boat, you will be able to brave any storm life throws your way.

3

Why Do Storms Come? Part 1

⟴◆⟴

An Unfortunate Accident

It was a late Sunday afternoon. I was sitting in the church's fellowship hall with ten other kids, waiting for youth group to start. I was talking and goofing off like any other normal tenth grader. While I was trying to impress one of the girls, I heard the door to the fellowship hall open. I watched as our youth pastor came in with tears in his eyes. He sat us all down in a circle, wiped his eyes, and with a slight shake in his voice, said, "Guys, I have some news for you, and this is not going to be easy." He paused for a moment, took a deep breath, and continued, "Steven was killed in a car accident this weekend."

We sat there in utter shock. Steven was in eleventh grade. He was an all-star athlete, an honor student, and an active member of our youth ministry. But most importantly, he was our close friend. We didn't know what to say. We didn't know what to do. We just sat there frozen. Frozen by confusion. Frozen by hurt. Frozen by anger. The room became eerily quiet. Then one of the girls broke the silence. "How? How did the accident happen?"

Our youth pastor composed himself and explained, "Steven and a couple of his friends went to a party this weekend. There was drinking, but from what I was told, Steven didn't have any alcohol. About two a.m., he and his friends left the party. They piled into the car; Steven sat in the back, and the owner, who had too much to drink, drove . They pulled out of the parking lot and headed down Middle Beach Road. As they were approaching a red light, the driver sped through the light, and a truck crossing the intersection crashed into them at full speed, and … Steven's life was taken."

We just sat there with dejected spirits. Broken. Despondent. Perplexed. Once again, no one said a word. The silence was deafening. We sat staring at each other for the longest time. Seconds felt like minutes, and the minutes felt like hours. Then a small voice broke the silence. "Pastor Jeff, why did this happen? Why did God do this?"

Is God Really To Blame?

This is the question of all time when tragedy strikes: Why did God do this? The first thing we want to do when a storm comes our way is find someone to blame. We usually point our finger at God, making him the main culprit, but is God always the one who causes the storms in our lives? Isn't God punishing us for the sin in our lives? The ancient Jews certainly believed that if something bad happened to them, it was the punishing wrath of God. We read stories, such as Sodom and Gomorrah where God burned the cities down with fire (Genesis 19:24), and we cannot ignore the fact that God sent a deluge that flooded the world because of wickedness in Genesis 7. However, does this mean that God still pours out his wrath every time we get out of line? Is God still to blame for every single affliction we experience?

There is a story in John that talks about how Jesus healed a blind man:

> Walking down the street, Jesus saw
> a man blind from birth. His disciples
> asked, "Rabbi, who sinned: this man
> or his parents, causing him to be born

blind?" Jesus said, "You're asking the wrong question. You're looking for someone to blame. There is no such cause-effect here. Look instead for what God can do. We need to be energetically at work for the One who sent me here, working while the sun shines. When night falls, the work day is over. For as long as I am in the world, there is plenty of light. I am the world's light." He said this and then spit in the dust, made a clay paste with saliva, rubbed the paste on the blind man's eyes, and said, "Go, wash at the Pool of Siloam" (Siloam means "sent"). The man went and washed—and saw (John 9: 1–7 MSG).

The disciples demanded an answer. "This has got to be someone's fault. Surely God is punishing this man for some sin, either he or his family did. Who's sin is it, Jesus?" However, Jesus basically tells them, "There is no blame to be given. It is no one's fault. Quit looking at God as the problem and start looking at him for the solution. "This happened so that the work of God might be displayed in his life" (John 9:3 MSG). And what was that work? Well, we know it wasn't infirmity and sickness. The work of God was healing and restoration!

Luke also tells us of a story in which people tried to blame God for an unfortunate catastrophe. In Jesus' day, there was a construction project that went wrong. A high tower that was being worked on fell, killing eighteen people. Once again, people tried to put the blame on God. So Jesus answers them in the form of a question, "Do you think those killed by the tower were more guilty than all the others living in Jerusalem? I tell you, no!" (Luke 13:4) Once again, Jesus tells them that no one is at fault. God didn't purposely knock over the tower to prove some grueling punitive point. However, Jesus uses this event to teach about repentance, an opportunity to turn to God; an opportunity to stop looking at God as the source of all calamities but rather as the consolation for our lives.

GUARDIANS OF CREATION

So if God is not the one to blame for the storms in our lives, where do they come from? Why are they here? I think we have to go back all the way to the beginning of Genesis to find our answer. God made the world ideal. It was a perfect place. God called his creation "good." In this good, perfect place, there was no pain, no suffering, and no tragedy; just a beautiful, peaceful utopia. All was harmonious.

Out of the dust, God created humanity, and made both the man and the woman in his image.

He blessed them and gave them a purpose to take care of his perfect, beautiful world. Genesis 2:15 states, "And the Lord God took man and put him in the garden of Eden to dress it and keep it." The woman was created to help man with this task of dressing (working) and keeping God's creation. I believe this was a mutual duty. I think it is amazing that God doesn't make woman from the head of man for her to rule over man, or makes her from the foot of man so that Adam can walk all over her. Instead, God makes her out of the side of man, from his rib, to walk beside him and be his partner. As Genesis 2:21–22 says, "So the LORD God made him fall into a deep sleep, and he took out one of the man's ribs. Then after closing the man's side, the LORD made a woman out of the rib." Men and women are to complete and complement each other. It was never about a power trip between genders. It has always been about equality among human beings, with God being the superior. God then gives dominance to both the male and the female. God confirms this by saying, "They will have power over the fish, the birds, and all animals, domestic and wild, large and small. So God created human beings, making them to be like Himself. He created them male and female" (Genesis 1:26–27). God equally created male and female. God wants both man and woman to work, rule, and keep his creation.

In Genesis 2:15, God tells humanity, concerning creation, that they are to "dress it and keep it." The word *keep* is the Hebrew word *shawmar,* which means "to guard and protect." So God calls humans the gatekeepers and guardians of his creation. They are the defense! The protective walls! The shining gates! But in God's perfect world, what does creation need protection from? God not only gave humans the ability to rule, work, and protect creation, but he gave them the ability to choose. God allows men and women to freely choose to love him or not, to follow him or turn away, which allows people to have an authentic love relationship with God. He blesses them with free will, not some divine mandate that forces them to follow him. In order for people to exercise free will, God must give them the ability to choose. He did this by planting a tree in the middle of the garden and then commanding them not to eat of this tree.

However, we have to ask ourselves, what was the real sin? Was it really about not eating from a tree? I think we find our answer in Genesis 3:1–4. Satan, disguised as a serpent, came to the woman and said:

> Did God really say, "You can't eat from any tree in the garden"? The woman answered the serpent, "We may eat the fruit from the trees in the garden.

But about the fruit of the tree in the middle of the garden, God said, 'You must not eat it or touch it or you will surely die.' " "No! You will not die!" the serpent said to the woman. "In fact, God knows that when you eat it, your eyes will be opened and you will be like God, knowing good from evil."

Notice that Satan tells her that "you will be like God"! There, for the first time, humanity saw the potential of making itself into God. Humans began to wonder: What would it be like to take the divine throne? What would it be like to be the final authority over everything?

Genesis 3:6 tells us, "Then the woman saw that the tree was good ..." What was once forbidden was now desirable, and by breaking God's law, humanity began to lust for absolute power. Humans bought into the lies of the Enemy. They exercised their free will. They let down their defenses. They disobeyed God, ate the fruit, and eventually sin was able to break through creation's protective gates. Corruption entered into creation.

SIN'S EPIDEMIC OUTBREAK

Evil quickly began to disrupt God's ideal world, and humans became filled with greed, lust, pride, evil, and shame. Sin soon spread like a deadly viral outbreak, invading God's creative order to the core, and the earth became cursed. God said to Adam, "You listened to your wife's voice and ate from the tree which I commanded you, 'Do not eat from it.' Cursed is the ground because of you ..." (Genesis 3:17). Paul affirms this by saying, "The creation itself will be set free from the bondage of corruption into the glorious freedom of God's children. For we know that the whole creation has been groaning together with labor pains until now ..." (Romans 8:21–22).

Paul tells us that all of creation is in bondage to corruption. Why? Because the earth became cursed as a result of Adam's sin. So the world turned from a place of peace to a place of chaos, from a place of life to a place of death, from a place of vitality to a place of infirmity, and from a place of idealness to a place of corruption. We witness the "groaning of creation" whenever disease strikes a body, a hurricane forces its violent winds upon a state, a famine strikes a nation, a flood sweeps through a neighborhood, an earthquake shakes a city, or when a tsunami strikes its intense power on a coastal town.

GOD'S REMEDY

One day, God will silence the destructive powers of nature. He will restore this corrupt world back to a peaceful utopia. We wait for the day that John saw in Revelation, "Then I saw a new heaven and a new earth, for the first heaven and the first earth had passed away" (Revelation 21:1). John goes on to tell us, "He will wipe every tear from their eyes. There will be no more death or mourning or crying or pain, for the older order of things has passed away" (Revelation 21:4).

God started restoring creation by first finding a remedy for humanity. This is important because humans are the guardians, the prize of God's creation. We are His beloved! However, the disease of sin separates humans from God, and since God is the source of all life, the penalty of sin always leads to death (Romans 6:23). So the only way that God can make an antidote for sin is through a blood sacrifice (Leviticus 17:11). In other words, someone has to die. But there is one problem: Everyone in creation has become infected by sin's deadly toxins. Since everyone is corrupted by sin, no one's blood is pure enough to be the antidote.

There is, however, one being who has never been exposed to sin's deadly outbreak, one who has never been infected, and one who has never carried the disease. This one is God! Yet, how does an eternal, immortal, and all powerful God die? There is only one way: He must become human. And this is exactly what he did. God, through his power and wisdom, did the impossible and willingly became flesh and blood. This human who was never infected by sin, lovingly gave his life as God's antidote to sin.

God prescribes this medicine to humanity through belief in Jesus. Why? Because Jesus is the cure. Jesus solved the problem. Jesus is God's only remedy for sin's deadly outbreak. Jesus finally heals the broken relationship between God and humanity. As Paul tells us, "Now we are set right with God by means of this sacrificial death, the consummate blood sacrifice. There is no longer a question of being at odds with God in any way. If, when we were at are worst, we were put on friendly terms with God by the sacrificial death of his Son …"(Romans 5:9–10 MSG). We do not have to be infected anymore. We do not have to live a life of spiritual sickness. We do not have to be separated from God. Every day, come to Jesus, and he will freely provide you with medicine to fight against the deadly disease of sin.

4

Why Do Storms Come? Part 2

⟫◆⟪

GOD PLEADS WITH HUMANITY

Ever since the beginning, God has been trying to restore humanity back to its rightful position of not only protecting creation but also enjoying a life with him. However, humans keep rejecting God. God has a right way to restore his creation, but humans think they have a better way. God gives them rules to help guide them, but humans would rather choose disobedience. God wants to show his love, but humans would rather love being God. God wants to remind humans that they are unique and made in his image, but they would rather make God into their image. This is why God continually pleads with humanity, "If my people, who are called by my name, will humble themselves and pray and seek my face and turn from their wicked ways, then I will hear from heaven and will forgive them their sin and will heal their land" (2 Chronicles 7:14).

In Jesus, God made this first step toward us. "But God demonstrates his own love for us in this, while we were still sinners, Christ died for us" (Romans 5:8). However, we need to make the next step and receive his gift of grace. When we do this, God will restore us, but it's our choice. It's the same choice Joshua had to make. "If serving the Lord seems undesirable to you, then choose for yourselves this day whom you will serve ... But as for me and my household, we will serve the Lord" (Joshua 24:15). Joshua wasn't going to let others decide for him. He did not let others be the determining factor in his life. He chose what he believed was right. He chose salvation. He chose God. God was able to use Joshua to win many difficult battles, all because Joshua was willing to freely choose God's way.

THE CHOICES WE MAKE

If we think about it, it really all comes down to choice. Do we choose right, or do we choose wrong?

Do we choose light, or do we choose the darkness? Do we choose God's plan, or do we choose our own? Yes, God gives us free will, but free will without responsibility always leads to chaos. Just because we have freedom, doesn't mean doing whatever we want is the better way. We need to follow God's way of freedom. God's way is always the right choice because God's purpose is always good, hopeful, and prosperous. Jeremiah 29:11 reminds us of this, " 'For I know the plans I have for you,' declares the Lord, 'plans to prosper you and not to harm you, plans to give you hope and a future.' "

GOD'S CHOICES ARE BETTER

Last time I checked, God is all-knowing, and we are not. God knows the entire future, and we usually have a hard time figuring out what to wear the next day. Can we really say that the choices we make in life are better than God's? Proverbs 14:12 states, "There is a way that seems right to a man but its end is the way of death [ruin]."

We always think we know better, but because we are not all-knowing, we usually make wrong decisions. That is why it is so important that we trust and acknowledge God in our choices. Proverbs 3:5–6 reminds us of this principle, "Trust in the Lord with all your heart, and do not rely on your own understanding; think about Him in all your ways, and He will guide you on the right paths."

Why did my friend Steven die in a car accident? Was it God's punishment? Is God to blame? I don't think so. I think it really came down to a matter of choice. The driver of the car chose to drink too much. He then chose to get behind the wheel. Then the driver chose to speed away. One bad decision led to another bad decision which then led to a fatal consequence. His decision not only affected himself but the others in the car with him.

We need to remember that our choices have consequences, and those consequences have repercussions to ourselves and everyone around us. We do not have the luxury to live in a safe, secure, and ideal world, so we must be wise concerning the choices we make. Have we really ever thought about how damaging each one of our wrong choices can be? Consider with me the following story about Billy.

BILLY'S STORY

Billy is in grade school and goes to a religious school. His teachers and administrators choose to see God as wrathful and punishing rather than loving and forgiving. Every time Billy makes a mistake, he gets hit by one of his teachers. His parents, who claim to be Christians, also see God as a punisher and choose to beat Billy every time he slips up. Billy decides that God must be mean and cruel; therefore, he wants nothing to do with God. He develops a deep hatred toward him.

As Billy grows up, he begins to see himself as worthless because he no longer sees himself in the image of his Creator. He develops low self-esteem and chooses to bully other kids to make himself feel better. As a bully, his peers began to despise him, and his father chooses physical abuse to help correct his son.

At eighteen, Billy chooses to drop out of school, move out of his house, and get a low-paying job. He finally feels so rejected, guilty, hurt, and confused by what has happened to him that he decides to turn to alcoholism to desensitize his inward scars. He goes from bar to bar to find comfort at the bottom of a bottle. At the bar, he meets a woman, and they eventually get married and have a child. Life becomes very hard for them. They never have enough money to pay the bills, and he is always getting fired. His wife thought she could change him, but he won't change. She keeps trying to help him, but he rejects her. He feels like she is always nagging him, telling him what to do. He chooses to resent her and begins to abuse his family physically and emotionally.

Billy decides to go back to the bar every night to escape the raging storm that has come upon his life. One night, he notices an attractive woman.

She is sweet and kind to him. He feels like he can connect with her better than he can with his own wife. He chooses to rent a hotel room, and he and this woman start having an affair. His wife eventually finds out about the affair; she moves out, taking the child with her. Eventually, their marriage ends in divorce, and Billy never sees his wife or child again.

Billy continues to blame God for his misery. Since he has such a miserable life, he continues to convince himself that God is mean and hateful. He lives the rest of his life drunk, alone, and angry.

ONE WRONG CHOICE

No one ever wakes up in the morning and decides, "Hey, I really would like to destroy my life today." It happens when we make one wrong choice after another. For Billy, it went all the way back to grade school when his teachers made a wrong decision about God. How differently might his life have turned out if the school and his parents saw God as loving and compassionate? What if Billy chose not to drop out of high school, turn to alcoholism, or to cheat on his wife? How much differently would his life have been? Did God want this life for Billy or his family? No. God's plans are good and prosperous (Jeremiah 29:11). At any point, Billy could have turned to God, but he chose to reject God instead. He could have turned to the light, but he preferred to stay in the darkness.

We need to remember that every decision we make can have dire consequences in the future. Most of the evil and suffering in the world today is caused by bad, wicked decisions. These bad decisions have led our world into war, economic downfalls, terrorism, environmental disasters, and corrupt governments. God is pleading with us to get it right. God wants us to start making good decisions and stop contaminating his planet with bad ones. God wants us to turn to him for the solution.

WHY DOESN'T GOD JUST REMOVE ALL EVIL?

Could God just remove all suffering and evil from the world? The simple answer would be yes, but how do you do that without affecting free will? If God was to remove evil, he then would have to remove *all* evil, including evil thoughts. This would limit humans' ability to freely think for themselves to choose either good or evil. This would discredit humanity to ever having any authentic love relationship with God. This is why God chose to send Jesus to the earth—so that we can choose Jesus and be restored to a loving relationship with God. Paul confirms this when he writes, "Even when we were God's enemies, he made peace with us, because his Son died for us. Yet something even greater than friendship is ours. Now that we are at peace with God, we will be saved by His Son's life" (Romans 5:10). As we follow Jesus, God continually teaches us how to make good, wholesome, and right decisions. The more good decisions we make, the less evil there will be in our world.

God's Power And Grace

I remember one of the songs at Steven's funeral was "Surely the presence of the Lord is in this place." The second line to the song says, "I can feel his mighty power and his grace." Every time I hear this hymn, it takes me back to that day. I remember the sorrow I felt, but it also reminds me that we can always find the strength to overcome anything in our lives. Why? Because even though we become overwhelmed by our storms, God never does!

When we rely on his power and grace, He gives us victory. "But thanks be to God, who gives us the victory through our Lord Jesus Christ" (1 Corinthians 15:57). Let this passage remind you that no matter what storm you are going through, you are already victorious. This isn't just a victory; it is supernatural victory! This is the victory that God has already given to you. Every day, we should wake up and thank God for all our victories, past, present, and future. We should tell God, "God, I know all I see right now is this storm surrounding me, but I also know that you are with me in this storm! Since you are with me, you have already given me victory during the storm, over the storm, and through the storm. Thank you, God, for allowing me to experience this with you so I can see your mighty power at work in my life."

During our storms, we need to continually be in an attitude of praise. Why? God always gets energized when we start thanking him for our situations, whether good or bad. When this happens, he quickly starts working on our behalf to bring overcoming power to our stormy situations.

5

Preparing For Storms

———◁◆▷———

HURRICANE SEASON

Florida is known for many things: sandy beaches, vacation spots, and Disney World. However, Florida is also known for hurricanes. Many people jokingly say, "Florida doesn't have any seasons." I have to disagree with them. Florida has three seasons: tourist season, snowbird season, and hurricane season.

Although we welcome the first two seasons, we never like the last one. Hurricane season puts Florida on high alert from June to November. In 2004, southern Florida was threatened by two ferocious hurricanes: Frances and Jeanne. I remember watching the Weather Channel and seeing the dark red-and-yellow swirls moving closer and closer to my state. The meteorologists kept telling us weeks before the first storm, Frances, launched its attack on the East Coast; "Now is the time to prepare. Start making your preparations today." As days grew closer, people started taking that advice.

As I drove around my city, the first thing I noticed was how many people were lined up at the gas stations. Every single pump was taken, and the cars were lined up all the way out into the road. Most people waited hours to fill their tanks, and stations quickly ran out of fuel. The stores were not any better. I remember walking into Home Depot and hundreds of people were buying generators and plywood for their windows. They literally cleared out Home Depot and other home repair stores had backorders for such items. In Walmart and Walgreens, you were be lucky if you could find any bottled water, batteries, or flashlights. People were preparing! People were getting ready! Why? Because that is what you do when a storm is approaching. You prepare.

PAY ATTENTION TO WARNINGS

The meteorologist is not the only one who warns about preparing for unexpected storms. The Bible makes the same warning about life. Proverbs 27:12

tells us, "A prudent person foresees danger and takes precautions. The simpleton goes blindly on and suffers the consequences." The questions we have to ask ourselves are, "What precautions have I made to protect myself from unexpected storms in life? How am I going to protect myself during an economic recession? How am I going to protect myself when I face health concerns? What will I do when I lose a loved one? What if I do something wrong and have guilt and shame?"

The first thing to do is to foresee danger. We need to remember that although living in safety and security is ideal, it just is not reality. We live in a world of turmoil, and we cannot ignore it. I am not saying live your life in fear, but what I am saying is, do not be the simpleton who walks blindly around thinking that every day will be perfect. This is not the case. If we can foresee danger, we will better know how to prepare against it. Just take time to prepare, and when the storm shows up, you will be ready to face it head-on.

BUILDING MATERIALS

The second thing to do is protect. How do we protect ourselves from storms? The answer lies in the teachings of Jesus. In Matthew 7:24–25, Jesus explains, "These words I speak to you are not incidental additions to your life, homeowner improvements to your standard of living. They are foundational words, words to build a life on. If you work these words into your life, you are like a smart carpenter who built his house on solid rock. Rain poured down, the river flooded, a tornado hit—but nothing moved that house. It was fixed to the rock."

Here, Jesus lays it out. The Bible isn't just a book of beautiful poetry and inspirational words to put you in a good mood. It's the concrete, wood, nails, and rebar that holds your life together. So how do we use these tools? Simply by hearing and responding. Jesus said to "work these words into your life." That means, we need to actually take the time every day to read, learn, understand, and put into practice the principles of God's Word.

START NOW

I know what you are thinking. "Alex, I don't have the time! It will be too much work!" Let me ask you this, Do you think the next storm that is developing and brewing out there is waiting for you to get your act together? Do you think the storm will give you sympathy because you do not have the "time" to prepare? Storms do not call in and make an appointment. They do not say, "Hey, how does Monday work for you? How about we meet at two in the afternoon?"

We cannot sit around and wait for the storm to catch us off guard. Now is the time to start thinking about preparations. Now is the time to get ready. Now is the time to start planning an evacuation route. We cannot wait for tomorrow or the next day, the next week, or next month. We need to start today! That's why the writer of Hebrews tells us, "Today, if you hear his voice, do not harden your hearts" (Hebrews 3:15).

THE FARMER

There is an old story about a farmer who waited too long to prepare for a storm. A heavy rain had been falling as a man drove down a lonely road. As he rounded a curve, he saw an old farmer surveying the ruins of his barn. The driver stopped his car and asked what had happened.

"Roof fell in," said the farmer. "Leaked so long, it finally just rotted through."

"Why in the world didn't you fix it before it got that bad?" asked the stranger.

"Well, sir," replied the farmer, "it just seemed I never did get around to it. When the weather was good, there weren't no need for it, and when it rained, it was too wet to work on!"

I think many times we ask ourselves the same question, "Why did I wait so long? Why didn't I fix this mess before it got so bad?" Let's not be the farmer, who was too busy in life to repair his roof before the storm came. By the time he needed a repaired roof, it was too late. We cannot be like the farmer who just didn't pay attention to the dangers of the weather. We need to start preparing today because we do not know what will come tomorrow. We have to ask ourselves, "Have I become too worried about God *preventing* my every storm that I am not willing to let Him *prepare* me for any storm?"

6

The Power Of God's Word

---∗◆∗---

POWER

So how does God's Word help us prepare for the storms of life? The first thing we need to understand is that God's Word has power! If God can speak into a chasm of chaos and darkness and create everything, can you imagine what God can do if we are willing to let him speak into the chasms of our lives? Remember, in Mark 4:39, it took Jesus just three words to bring peace to a raging storm, "Quiet! Be still!" That's power! That's God's Word!

Terminated

A few years ago, I witnessed the power of God's Word in my life. I was a youth director at a medium-sized church in Stuart, Florida. It was a Monday morning, and I was sitting at my desk, preparing for the staff meeting. At that moment, the senior pastor and the business administrator stepped into the office, shut the door, and sat down. The pastor looked at me very solemnly and said, "Alex, we need to talk to you."

"Is everything okay?" I asked.

With stern looks, they placed a typewritten piece of paper on my desk. When I picked it up, I couldn't believe what was at the top: THIS IS A NOTICE OF TERMINATION OF EMPLOYMENT. I just stared at it in horror. Is this really happening? Is this a bad dream? I placed the notice back on the desk. All I could say was, "Why?"

The pastor responded, "Alex, we have two different visions for this youth ministry. I am sorry, but you have till the end of the day to clear out your office." Then both men got up from their chairs, opened the door, and walked out.

For the next few years, I worked in a window-cleaning business. The hours were horrible, I barely made enough money to pay my bills, and my bank account was quickly diving into the red. At this time, I was forced to leave the apartment I was renting and was taken in by a friend.

Discouragement and despair crept into my life. I spent many countless nights crying out to God. I thought I had failed him in ministry and that he had kicked me out! Over and over, thoughts of worry and doubt raced through my mind. Was I ever going to be able to fulfill God's call for me? Did God really give up on me? How could I have failed God so badly? These thoughts haunted me night after night.

One night, as I was wallowing in my misery and asking God for an answer, I heard the Holy Spirit speak to my heart, "Philippians 1:6. Turn to Philippians 1:6." Wiping my eyes, I picked up my Bible and flipped open to Paul's letter to the Philippians. When I skimmed down to chapter one verse six and couldn't believe what I read: "Being confident of this, that He who began a good work in you will carry it on to completion until the day of Christ Jesus."

I just sat there with my mouth hanging open. God was speaking to me! He was encouraging me! He was saying, "Alex, I have not given up on you." Every day for a year, I read this passage, remembered this passage, and spoke this passage over my life. I could feel God strengthening my heart and building up my faith. I knew the time of my deliverance was coming, but I just wasn't sure when.

Then one day it happened. God gave me this vision for a discipleship program. I grabbed a piece of paper and started jotting down everything that came to my heart and mind. I worked diligently on this every day for a year. I had my sister help me put a proposal together and made an appointment to visit the senior pastor of the church I was attending.

I sat down in his office and shared with him the vision that God placed on my heart. He looked at me with a big smile and said, "Alex, this is what we need to be doing. One day, you will be hired here."

How long had I waited to hear those words? His words spoke hope and life into my darkened spirit. It's like after a bad thunderstorm when you see that glimmer of sunlight shining through the black clouds—you know it's going to be a better day. I wasn't hired on the spot, but eventually the church did bring me on the pastoral staff as the full-time Director of Discipleship. God was fulfilling his promise to me. He finally was continuing the "good work" that he began in me.

GOD'S WORD SUCCEEDS

God's Word has power in our lives. Why? Because when God speaks, he accomplishes! "So my word that goes out from my mouth: It will not return to me empty, but will accomplish what I desire and achieve the purpose for which I sent it"(Isaiah 55:11).

God's Word has the wisdom to prepare you for any storm life might throw at you. However, keeping His word tucked away nicely on the shelf to collect dust is like keeping hurricane shutters locked in the garage when a category four storm is about to strike or not seeking an underground shelter when a tornado is about to rip through your town. The psalmist knew the protecting power of God's word when he wrote, "I have hidden your word in my heart that I might not sin against you" (Psalm 119:11). There was a danger called sin that kept lurking around the psalmist's heart. He paid attention to the warnings and sheltered his heart with God's word. Every day, we have situations, problems, and hurts that lurk around our hearts. Let's look at some examples of how God's Word can protect us against life's storms.

ECONOMIC STORMS

When financial storms hit, they hit us hard. We watch as our bank accounts start to drift away and our investments begin to erode. We become worried and wonder, how did this happen? What I am going to do? What will the future be like? So what are some ways God's word protect us from such storms? Proverbs 13:11 states, "Dishonest money dwindles away, but he who gathers money little by little makes it grow." The Bible's principle for saving tells us to gather money "little by little to make it grow." The Bible teaches that one way to protect ourselves from economic storms is to start saving our money right now. In other words, "save for a rainy day." We should continually search out new methods on how to save our money.

In Philippians 4:12, Paul teaches another principle to help us when financial storms start to develop: "I know what it is to be in need, and I know what it is to have plenty. I have learned the secret of being content in any and every situation." In today's world, we are continually bombarded with advertisements saying, "You need the latest ..." "You have to have ..." "You can't live without ..." These statements are detrimental to our economic health. When we hear these statements, we should take time to think over our purchases and not buy on impulse. The key to this is learning contentment. Contentment is basically the ability to not have everything you want, or at least not to have it all at once. This doesn't mean that you cannot have nice things; it just means you will think twice before making your next purchase.

Worry is another factor. Worry is telling God, "I don't think you can do it because I don't see how you can." Faith is the opposite. Faith is telling God, "I don't see how you can do it, but I know you can." Jesus advises, "So do not worry, saying, 'What shall we eat?' or 'What shall we drink?' or 'What shall we wear?' For the pagans run after all these things, and your heavenly Father knows that you need them. But seek first his kingdom and his righteousness, and all these things will be given to you as well" (Matthew 6:31–33). Jesus tells us to stop focusing on the natural and begin focusing on the supernatural. God knows what you need every day, and he will take care of it for you. Remember, God knows your finances. He knows them better than you do. He is your divine accountant. Keep your focus on him, and he will guide you through all economic storms.

HEALTH STORMS

Health is also a major contributing factor when it comes to our lives. Well, it *is* our life. However, every day we face health concerns ranging from cancer, to diabetes, to weight control, to allergies, to the common cold, and so on. Unfortunately, this is the fallen world we live in. Creation is groaning. Sickness is a reality, and as a result, our bodies become infected. However, the Bible is very concerned about your health, probably because its author designed you as "fearfully and wonderfully made" (Psalm 139:14).

So how can the Bible's teaching help protect us from health problems? There is a story in Daniel, where Daniel and his three friends are participating in a royal banquet. The king offers Daniel and his friends the richest royal food of wine and meat. Daniel realizes that this food might not be the healthiest food for him and denies the king's royal meal. Daniel then says to the king's guard, "Please test your servants for ten days: Give us nothing but vegetables to eat and water to drink. Then compare our appearances with that of the young men who eat the royal food …" (Daniel 1:12–13). So, for ten days, Daniel and his friends ate a different diet than everyone else in the kingdom. "At the end of the ten days, they looked healthier and better nourished than any of the young men who ate the royal food" (Daniel 1:15). Did you catch that? They were "healthier and better nourished." Why? Because they made better decisions about their diets. They chose salads over hamburgers.

Now, I am not saying we all have to give up on meat and become vegetarians, but what I am saying is that maybe we should start making better decisions concerning what we eat and drink. Maybe instead of drinking soda all the time, we should drink more water. Maybe instead of eating cookies and chips, we should have carrots and celery sticks. Maybe we should trade white bread for whole wheat bread, and maybe fish and chicken is a better choice than steak and pork.

The Bible also teaches about the importance of exercise, "As the saying goes, exercise is good for the body …" (1 Timothy 4:8), seeking a doctor when we are sick, "Healthy people don't need a doctor, but sick people do" (Luke 5:31), and not polluting our bodies because they are the houses of God, "Don't you realize your body is a temple of the Holy Spirit?" (1 Corinthians 6:19).

Prayer also plays an essential role in our health. We should never underestimate the power of prayer. Prayer reminds us that we have a God who "forgives all our sins and heals all our diseases" (Psalm 103:3). Whenever we are starting to feel sickness invade our physical health, we should always call and make an appointment with the Great Physician.

GRIEF STORMS

Death is a part of life. There is nothing more lonely or bitter than the cold rains of death and grief. We are usually left hopeless and questioning, "Why did they have to die? How can I bear the loss of my loved one? Will I ever see them again?" The best protection for death is hope—hope in knowing that we have a Savior who conquered death. This Savior declared, "I am the resurrection and the life. He who believes in me will live, even though he dies" (John 11:25). This is the hope we have in Jesus. He is the only one who ever conquered death and left the grave perplexed when he rose on the third day. This is why Paul exclaimed, "O death, where is your victory? O death, where is your sting?" (1 Corinthians 15:55 NIV). Since death has been defeated, it cannot hold us to the grave for eternity. We have hope! A hope in an eternity! A hope in a resurrected life! A hope in a living Savior! A hope in the promise, "Because I live, you also will live" (John 14:19b).

Jesus understands death. He understands what it means to lose someone close to you. He knows what you are going through. He was there at his friend Lazarus's funeral, and he cried for him (John 11:45). The Bible says, "He was deeply moved in spirit and troubled" (John 11:35). When death comes and takes the one we love, it is okay for us to feel "deeply moved in spirit and troubled." This is the grieving process.

But try not to tackle the storms of grief by yourself. Come to God. Jesus said, "Blessed are those that mourn, for they will be comforted" (Matthew 5:4). Allow God to comfort you during your time of grief. Dive into the loving arms of the Savior, talk to him about the pain you are enduring, and share with him the grief you are experiencing. He will be there every step of the way, reminding you that he hasn't abandoned you and will exchange your anguish for his peace. A supernatural peace that will "guard your heart and mind" (Philippians 4:7). In time, this peace will calm the restless wind and waves of your soul.

RELATIONSHIP STORMS

If anyone knew about relationships, it was Jesus. The man thrived on relationships. He had a close network of friends. He healed people out of compassion. He ate dinner with people who were despised. He had deep conversations with people who were outcasts. Jesus loved relationships, and he wants us to have good relationships also.

However, sometimes relationships can go bad, and we are severed from the ones we love. Jesus taught us some principles on how to restore broken relationships. In Matthew 18:15, Jesus tells us, "If a fellow believer hurts you, go and tell him—work it out between the two of you. If he listens, you've made a friend." Jesus is telling us that we can't sit this one out.

The first step to restoring a relationship is by rejuvenating a relationship. Rejuvenating means to make new again. Jesus is not saying, "Go around telling everyone how that person hurt you." Rather, he is saying, "Go and try to breathe new life into your broken relationships." Jesus says, "Work it out between the two of you." In other words, you need to find a way to be on speaking terms again with that person.

Jesus also tells us that we need to forgive each other. Matthew 6:12 states, "And forgive us our sins, as we have forgiven those who sin against us." Forgiveness is the key when it comes to restoring a relationship. For one thing, you are not bound by bitterness anymore. Unforgiveness is a poison that eats away at your mind, body, and soul, slowly causing you to shut down. I heard this saying before, "Unforgiveness is like sitting across from your enemy, drinking poison, and expecting the other person to die." Unforgiveness is being locked up in a prison, waiting to be executed. Forgiveness is the key to freedom. Forgiveness brings life and lifts the burden of the soul.

However, forgiveness is not always easy. This is why Jesus tells us, "Pray for those who hurt you" (Matthew 5:44b). If you are having trouble forgiving somebody, first start by praying God's blessing upon their life. Ask God to help you forgive this person. Rely on God's strength and grace. Ask God to give you the opportune time to talk with this person. Every time we have trouble forgiving someone, we need to look at Jesus and ask ourselves, "Is there anything that someone can do to me that hasn't already been done to him?" Remember, while Jesus was being beaten, humiliated, and tortured on the cross, he somehow had the compassion and love to say, "Father God, forgive them ..."(Luke 23:34). If Jesus could do this while being crucified, surely he can give us the strength to forgive those who hurt us.

GUILT STORMS

We need to realize that none of us are perfect. We all make mistakes. The Bible tells us, "There is no one who always does what is right, not even one" (Romans 3:10). That means, we all have blown it. We are all in this together. There is nothing bad that you have done that someone else hasn't already done. This is why Jesus came. Jesus wasn't coming to find good and righteous people; he came to save sinners like you and me. "For the Son of Man came to find and restore the lost" (Luke 19:10 MSG). God isn't up in heaven, looking down on you, saying, "Oh, wow. You messed up again! What I am going to do with you? How could you disappoint me like that? Now you are really going to get it!" No. God lovingly reminds us, "For it is by God's grace that you have been saved through faith. It is not the result of your own efforts, but God's gift, so that no one can boast about it" (Ephesians 2:8).

The Bible also tells us, "There is therefore now no condemnation for those who are in Christ Jesus" (Romans 8:1). Since Jesus came to save us, we are free from guilt! We do not have to keep reliving past mistakes over and over again. We can, "confess our sins; he is faithful and just to forgive us our sins and to cleanse us from all unrighteousness" (1 John 1:9). Why is all of this possible? The answer is simple, "God showed his great love for us by sending Christ to die for us while we were still sinners. And since we have been made right in God's sight by the blood of Christ, he will certainly save us from God's condemnation" (Romans 5:8).

The storm is coming. Are you ready? How have you prepared yourself? I think now is the best time to go to the shelf and dust off the main thing that will protect you from life's storms: God's Word!

7

During The Storm

⟫◆⟪

A Chance Of Survival

It was a sunny day in October, the weather was great, and I was driving with my fiancée over to her parents' house in Lakeland, Florida. We were having a discussion about God, life, and eternity, when all of a sudden, my fiancée started sobbing. I reached over and took her hand. I knew immediately what was wrong. Her parents didn't know God, and she wasn't sure about their eternal destination. I wasn't sure what to say or do, so I started to pray for her family. It was one of those rare times when God just hits you in the right spot, and you start feeling his presence alive in you. The words just came to me. I knew that God was up to something, but I didn't know what.

A couple of weeks later, we received a call from my fiancée's sister, Yun Jun. She told us that the doctors had diagnosed her with a rare and aggressive uterine cancer. Our hearts sank; we could see the dark clouds starting to form around us. We knew we needed to get ready to brace ourselves against the sullen, cold rains of fear and doubt. We couldn't understand why this was happening. Was this really what God was up to? What was he doing? So we just started praying, believing that God was going to heal her and bring peace to this situation.

A week later, we were devastated when Yun Jun called again from the hospital in Lakeland. My fiancée stood frozen as her sister told her, "The doctors said the cancer is very difficult to cure, and I have a fifty-fifty chance of survival."

My fiancée burst into tears and hit the floor like a rag doll. Now the rain was beginning to pour down on us. All we could see was darkness, and the wind was chipping away any hope that was in our hearts. I knelt down next to her and held her. It was one of those moments when you do not have the right words to say. I mean, what can you say? I asked her, "Do you want to go to Lakeland to see your sister?" When she looked up at me, she didn't have to say a word. I knew she wanted to go.

Eye of the Storm:

We packed up my truck and headed three hours north to Lakeland Regional Hospital As we entered Yun Jun's room, I sensed that God wanted us to pray over her. My fiancée and I gathered around her bed and asked God to remove the cancer.

Yun Jun had surgery the following week. The surgery was a success, and all traces of the cancer were gone! God came through!

A week later, we visited Yun Jun again in the hospital. She told us that she was in a lot of pain. In the hospital room was my fiancée, her parents, and me. Their mother asked, "Alex, will you please pray that God will take away the pain?" This was the first time that she ever mentioned prayer. I couldn't believe it. Was God actually starting to answer my prayer from two weeks ago? Were her parents starting to believe and have faith?

We stood, joined hands, and prayed over Yun Jun. This was the first time this family had ever prayed together. That Thanksgiving, the father had his family pray again. God was definitely up to something, and that something was good.

DARK CLOUDS

When the storm clouds are hanging over our heads, it is really hard to see anything but darkness. It's hard to notice any glimmer of light through the heavy dark clouds and the pelting rain. You feel alone, cold, and bleak, wondering, when is the sun

65

going to shine again? When am I going to feel its warmth? Are there blue skies on the horizon? The storm deceives us into thinking there is nothing but hopelessness and darkness.

If we were to look past the clouds, however, we would notice that the sun has not gone anywhere. It is still up there, shining, even if we can't see it. The same is true of God. When we are in desperate, painful situations, it is hard for us to see that God is there and is working. Just like the sun, he is still there, shining in all his glory.

God was up to something good in my fiancée's family, even though we couldn't actually see it. This means that God is also up to something good in your situation, even though *you* may not see it.

BEHIND THE SCENES

There is a story in 2 Kings 6 where Elisha and his servant are facing a terrible problem. The king was angry at them and sent an army to kill them both. I know, pretty harsh, right? Two against an entire army. Not fair, but that's the way it was, I guess. So:

> The servant of the man of God got up and went out early the next morning and an army with horses and chariots surrounded the city. "Oh my lord, what shall we do?" the servant

asked. "Don't be afraid," the prophet answered, "those who are with us are more than those who are with them." And Elisha prayed, "Oh Lord, open his eyes so he may see." Then the Lord opened the servant's eyes, and he looked and saw the hills full of horses and chariots of fire all around Elisha (2 Kings 6:15–17).

God is up to something. God is always working behind the scenes. Elisha didn't focus on the storm; Elisha focused on his God! He peered right through the dark storm clouds and saw God's army! He saw God because he had faith. "Faith is the evidence of what we do not see" (Hebrews 11:1).

ACTIVATING FAITH

Elisha then activated his faith through prayer. We too need to activate our faith through prayer. The Bible tells us, "Don't fret or worry. Instead of worrying, pray. Let petitions and praises shape your worries into prayers, letting God know your concerns" (Philippians 4:6). Instead of worrying and being afraid, Elisha prayed and believed. He knew that prayer allows God's supernatural power to penetrate our natural world. When he did this, he saw that God was strong enough to defeat his strongest enemy.

If God is strong enough to stop Elisha's enemies from advancing on him, surely he is strong enough to deliver you from the storm you are facing. Prayer always activates God's power in our lives!

STILL

We need to come to the realization that we are not strong enough to take on storms by ourselves. We need help! This is why God says, "Be still and know that I am God" (Psalm 46:10). Elisha certainly did this, and we should too. To be still means to rest in God's power during life's difficulties. We can always find safety in God during these storms. This is why Solomon wrote, "God's name is a place of protection, and good people can run there and be safe" (Proverbs 18:10 MSG).

EYE OF A HURRICANE

During a hurricane, the safest place to be (besides indoors) is in the center of the storm, known as the eye. In the eye, there is no wind, rain, or ominous dark cloud cover. Rather, it is a peaceful, sunny, and beautiful place. All around, torrential rains and powerful winds are wreaking havoc, but in the eye of the storm, you are in complete safety.

God is like the eye of a storm. All around you may be hell on earth, but in God, you will feel the peace of heaven. This is why David said, "I waited patiently for the Lord. He turned to me and heard my cry. He lifted me out of the slimy pit, out of the mud and mire" (Psalm 40:1–2). David continued to cry day and night for God to rescue him. He continually sought after God, and eventually his patience paid off. God delivered him out of his situation.

Sometimes going through the storm is painful, but if you are patient and still, you will witness the power of God. Stop focusing on the storm's destroying power, and start focusing on God's restoring power. When you begin to trust in God, he will show himself to you, and eventually, the storm will pass.

8

What Would God Say?

━━━◆━━━

Let's imagine for a moment that you are sitting across from God. You have questions concerning the storm you are going through. How would God answer you?

God, I feel so alone. Does anybody know what I am going through?

My child, you are not alone. I am always here with you. I promised you that I would "never leave you nor forsake you" (Hebrews 13:5). The reason you feel alone is because you are focusing so hard on your problem and not focusing on my presence. I want you to start shifting your focus to me, and I will start to bring healing to your situation. I became a human so I could feel the pain you are going through. I know what rejection feels like. I have cried over friends who have died. I have experienced humiliation. I know what it is like to be in poverty. I get it when people misunderstand you. I want you to remember "that I understand your weaknesses, for I faced all of the same testings as you do" (Hebrews 4:15).

God, I don't understand. Why is this happening to me?

My child, at the moment, you are not supposed to know why you are going through all of this, but later you will. "Right now you don't see things very clearly. You are squinting through a fog, peering through a mist. But it won't be long before the weather clears up and sun shines bright. You will see it all then, see it as clearly as I see it" (1 Corinthians 13:12). I am trying to steer you through this storm. If you knew what was happening to you, you might try to take the wheel and navigate through the treacherous waters, not knowing where you are going. Then you would be lost at sea. The important thing is, I have sailed these waters before, and I know how to get you out. I ask that you trust me because "I have it all planned out, plans to take care of you, not to abandon you, plans to give you the future you hoped for" (Jeremiah 29:11).

God, I feel so guilty. Do you still love me?

My child, I cannot help but love you. "I have lavished my love upon you" (1 John 3:1). This was why I became a human. Every time you question my love for you, look at Jesus. I came to restore a relationship with you by giving my life for you. I couldn't bear to see you suffer punishment. "So, I put my love on the line by offering myself as a sacrificial death" (Romans 5:8). Because of this, "my loyal love will not run out, my merciful love will not dry up, and my mercies are renewed every morning" (Lamentations 3:22–23). If you feel guilty, please understand this is not from me because "there is no condemnation for those who are in Christ" (Romans 8:1). All I ask is that you "just take time to talk with me, admit your sins, I won't let you down. I will forgive your sins and purge you from wrongdoing" (1 John 1:9). And always remember that "nothing can separate you from my love" (Romans 8:39).

God, are you even listening to me?

My child, I am "very attentive to your prayers" (1 Peter 3:12). I am always listening to you because I care deeply about what you have to say. I care about what you have to say because I so desperately want to be in a relationship with you. "I love you with an everlasting love and I have drawn you with lovingkindness" (Jeremiah 31:3). I love listening to you so much that "I will silence all of heaven just to hear you and store all your prayers in golden vessels; they are like a beautiful fragrance to me" (Revelation 8:1–3).

God, I can't take it anymore! How can I go on one more day?

My child, that's because you are relying too much on your own strength. If you would just rely on my power you would realize that "my grace is enough, it's all you need. My strength is made perfect in your weakness" (2 Corinthians 12:9). This means, "I know your weaknesses and I know them better than you do. I will be faithful to you, I will never let you be pushed past your limit, I will always be there to help you come through it" (1 Corinthians 10:13). I want you to take all your problems and give them to me. All I want you to do is to trust me. "Give your entire attention to what I am doing right now, and don't get worked up about what may or may not happen tomorrow. I will help you deal with whatever hard things come up when the time comes" (Matthew 6:34). Also remember, "you can do everything through Me because I will give you My strength" (Philippians 4:13).

9

The Aftermath

---×◆×---

REBUILDING

Eventually storms pass. The rain stops. The floodwaters recede. The wind dies down. The skies begin to clear. The sun comes out. Homes get repaired. Cities get rebuilt. Communities finally get restored.

Storms can leave us in ruins. Then we need to start putting our broken lives back together again. In many ways, we can feel like Nehemiah, who looked upon a destroyed city and said, "You see the trouble we are in: Jerusalem lies in ruins; and its gates have been burned with fire" (Nehemiah 2:17). After calamity strikes us, whether it is health, the economy, shame, or relationships, we feel like a city in ruins and wonder, "How am I going to put this life back together?" Well, I think we can find our answer in Nehemiah.

Nehemiah stands in front of all the people and proclaims, "Come, let us rebuild the wall of Jerusalem" (Nehemiah 2:18). Nehemiah didn't wallow in self-pity. He didn't hide in his house and ignore the disastrous situation. No. Nehemiah was ready and willing to change his situation. He knew he could make it better and was ready to get to work.

TIME TO MAKE A CHANGE

If you are going to come out of this storm you are in, you first have to be willing to change. No one can do this for you. It is totally up to you. If you want change, you need to *make* a change. However, it won't happen overnight. It may take some time for you to experience recovery. It took fifty-two days for Nehemiah to repair the wall (Nehemiah 6:15). We have to give God time to clean up the messes in our lives, but if we are patient and *willing*, he will. So are you ready to start rebuilding? Are you ready to get to work and restore the brokenness that the storm left behind? But you do not have to do it alone. God will be there every step of the way, helping, guiding, and restoring.

EARTHQUAKE STRIKES

In 2010, a massive 7.0 earthquake shook the Haitian capital Port-au-Prince to the core. How could we forget that day? We all felt the aftershocks of pain and suffering across the world from the Haitian people. We watched with tears as the networks broadcasted pictures and videos of the devastation. Immediately, nations, organizations, and faith-based groups pulled together to send relief effort to the country. Once again, people asked, "Where is God?"

Unfortunately, some made some hurtful assumptions that God was punishing the Haitian people because their ancestors made a "deal with the devil." Why do we have the tendency to see God in a negative light? I think this is why so many people struggle with storms of life because God is always seen as the problem and never the solution. We need to begin to make a radical change as to how we see God. We need to see him for who he really is: the *answer*, not the *problem*.

WHAT IS GOD UP TO?

Where was God during the 2010 earthquake in Haiti? What was he doing? Nehemiah tells us, "I answered them by saying, 'The God of heaven will give us success. We his servants will start building'" (Nehemiah 2:20). Nehemiah tells us that

God is in the rebuilding stage. Not only is God part of the relief effort, he is the reason it succeeds. God puts together groups of people to send relief to devastating areas where people desperately need aid. God uses people. God doesn't have any solo acts. God is team-oriented. Nehemiah states, "Let *us* start building" (Nehemiah 2:18b). He doesn't say, "Let *me* start rebuilding" or "You know what guys? I've got this." Nehemiah realizes that when it comes to rebuilding cities, communities, and people's lives, it takes a group effort.

Nehemiah couldn't do it alone, and when it comes to restoring your life, you can't do it alone either. Ask God to send the right people to help you. The Bible says, "Plans fail for a lack of counsel, but with many advisors they succeed" (Proverbs 15:22). Do not be afraid to listen to the advice of godly, loving people who desperately want to help you. However, make sure you are relying on God as your primary source of counsel, as the Bible reminds us, "First seek the counsel of the Lord" (1 Kings 22:5).

RESCUE

God is in the rescuing business. God will comfort you in your time of need and will always show up in the rescue unit. God cannot stand to leave people in a chaotic mess of despair. His Word tells us, "For he rescued us from the dominion of darkness" (Colossians 1:13), "he rescues us from the slimy pit, the mud and mire" (Psalm 40:2), and he rescues us from our enemies (Psalm 143:9). However, sometimes God's rescue plans do not make sense to us and seem confusing, but we need to remember that he is always faithful and strong to deliver (Psalm 144:2).

SHIPWRECKED

There is a story about a ship's captain from the 1800s who shipwrecked on a deserted island. One night his ship was caught in a major storm and it capsized. The only surviving member, he swam to the closest beach he could find. Stranded on this island, day after day he looked to the horizon for any passing ships.

Every once in a while, a ship passed by, but he was never successful in getting anyone's attention. The days went on. The days turned into weeks, and weeks turned into months. Every night, the man asked God to be rescued. The captain learned how to live off the land and even made a small hut to live in and store all his possessions. One night, while he was out fishing, a terrible thunderstorm pounded the island. He ran to a nearby cave and waited for the storm to pass. After several hours, the rain died down, and the sky cleared. He stepped out of the cave and walked toward his hut with his nightly catch. As drew closer to his hut, he noticed a bright, reddish-orange light bursting forth from the trees. He began to run, and the closer he got, he started to smell smoke. The man finally realized what had happened. Lightning had struck, causing a fire.

He finally made it to the place where his hut was, but was too late. His hut was on fire, and he watched as it burned to the ground. The man, overtaken by despair, just fell in the dirt and lay there. With tears in his eyes, he raised his voice to God, "Why, God? Why did you do this? This was the only home I have! Are you ever going to rescue me off this island? Do you even care?" Exhausted, the man fell asleep.

The next morning, he was awakened by the sound of voices coming from the beach. He jumped to his feet and looked down toward the shore. He saw three men standing on the beach, a small boat a few yards out, and a large ship in the distance. The man raced toward the shore and greeted the three men.

An elderly gentleman greeted him, "Good morning. Have you been here long? What happened to you?"

The man explained how he lost his ship a few months earlier and was stranded on this island. Then he looked at the gentleman and asked, "How did you know to come looking for me?"

The gentleman responded, "Well, last night we were a little past the horizon, when we saw your fire signal coming up over those trees. We realized that someone might be there and decided we would go check it out in the morning. So here we are."

What the man saw as tragedy, God used as strategy. The man thought he had lost everything because his hut burned down, but it was the light that God used to signal a rescue party. Just because we might not always understand God's methods, doesn't mean that we can't trust God's methods. All we need to know is that God is always faithful and will come to your aid every time. Paul tells us, "If we are faithless, he remains faithful, for he cannot disown himself" (2 Timothy 2:13b).

OVERPOWERING THE STORM

God wants you to be rescued and restored. God wants you to taste victory! This is why he calls you a champion over life's defeats. "No, in all these things we are more than conquerors through him who loved us" (Romans 8:37). God believes in you. The question is, do you believe in yourself? Do you believe in God's victorious power in your life? When life throws us challenges, we must come to realize that we cannot rely on our own strength but must rely on his. We come to recognize that God is not the one to be blamed but the one to be praised. When we finally realize this, we come to understand that God will give us supernatural power to overpower, overthrow, and overcome any storm we encounter.

We need to remember that God believes in us and calls us conquerors! When it comes to God, we need to stop blaming and start proclaiming. If Jesus spoke overcoming power to his storms, and his power lives within us, then we should speak overcoming power to our storms.

When family problems arise, proclaim, "I am a conqueror in Christ!"

When our country is in a recession, proclaim, "I am a conqueror in Christ!"

When the doctor's report comes in with a diagnosis, proclaim, "I am a conqueror in Christ!"

When the car breaks down, proclaim, "I am a conqueror in Christ!"

When depression and anxiety seeps in, proclaim, "I am a conqueror in Christ!"

When guilt and shame overwhelm, proclaim, "I am a conqueror in Christ!"

Proclaiming is not about manipulating God into doing something because we say some mystical biblical incantation. It is about getting our faith animated because we proclaim the Word of God over our lives. Faith comes by hearing God's Word (Romans 10:17).

Whatever the situation in life, you are always God's conqueror, ready to do battle, challenging the storm head-on, and declaring your victory!

Does this mean we will never struggle and that every storm will just pass us by? No, but what it does mean is that you are guarding your heart and mind against its bitter winds. You are starting to believe that you have the power of Jesus inside of you to rebuild, restore, and repair the brokenness of your life.

GAINING A NEW PERSPECTIVE

God teaches us two things in the aftermath of life's storms. One, we realize how much more resilient we are because of God's power. The winds and rains of life's storms tend to make our faith stronger. So the next time they show up, they won't seem so scary. James tells us, "Consider it pure joy whenever you face trials of many kinds, because you know that the testing of your faith develops perseverance" (James 1:2–3).

Perseverance is the ability to keep on going. It is never giving up, never giving in, and never backing down. Perseverance is that hope inside you, reminding you that no matter how dark the days are today, they will always be brighter tomorrow.

How is perseverance developed? It is developed through the trials of today. When our faith is tested, our perseverance grows stronger. God doesn't necessarily cause the storms in your life, but he will use them to make you a better person, helping you to live up to your fullest potential. The challenges you face today are going to shape your character for tomorrow.

In the aftermath of life's storms, we finally understand who God is during the storm. Our perspective begins to change, and we become aware of why these storms happened. We realize we have a God who comforts, guides, heals, provides, and forgives. If we never experienced sickness, how would we know God's healing power? If we never experienced poverty, how would we know that he provides? If we never grieved, how would we know that he comforts? If we have never had broken relationships, how do we know that he restores? If we never messed up, how would we experience his forgiveness? If we never faced loneliness, how would we know that he is a "friend that sticks closer than brother"? (Proverbs 18:24). The only way to know these things is by experiencing them, standing back, and being amazed by God's power.

Second, we began to empathize with people who are going through similar experiences. We realize, "Hey, I know what you are going through. I went through the same thing. Maybe I can help." This is why Paul says, "He comes alongside us when we go through hard times, and before you know it, he brings us alongside someone else who is going through hard times so that we can be there for that person just as God was there for us" (2 Corinthians 1:5 MSG). God will have you join his relief effort and begin to use you in mighty ways to help other people. Others who are going through the same storms you went through; others who have become confused, lonely, and hurt; and others who will need your support as you help them through life's treacherous waters.

IDENTIFYING JESUS

After Jesus calmed the storm, the disciples asked a very important question, "Who is this?" (Mark 4:41). The answer to that question will define how you stand against the storms of life. Who is Jesus to you? Is he the teacher who prepares you for the storm? Is he the shepherd who comforts you during the storm? Is he the Messiah who gives you peace in the storm? Is he the suffering servant who goes with you through the storm? Is he the God who commands the storm to be still?

When you feel the storms of life raging, who is Jesus to you?

10

Discussion

———⟫◆⟪———

Session 1

Q1. Do you agree with this statement, "Life is not fair"? Why or why not?

Q2. Why do you think bad things happen in life? Do you think God is to blame for all the evil in the world? Why or why not?

Q3. Read Psalm 72:12. How does one get delivered by God? What does this passage tell you about God in the midst of our tragedies?

Q4. Read Psalm 72:13. What is this passage telling you about God's feelings toward those who need help? What does this mean to you?

Q5. Read Psalm 72:14. What strikes you about this passage? How does God treat those who have been oppressed?

Q6. Read Psalm 69:1–3. Have you ever felt like the psalmist in this passage? Describe a time when God came to your rescue. How did he shown himself to you?

Q7. What do you want to learn from this study? What questions do you hope God will answer for you while you read this book?

Read chapter one, "Storms Will Come"

Session 2

Q1. Was there ever a time you found yourself in a horrible storm (hurricane, tornado, flood, thunderstorm, etc.)? What emotions did you feel? What were you thinking? Were you afraid or excited?

Q2. Why do you think we shouldn't be in denial when it comes to life's storms? What storms do you feel yourself struggling with right now (financial, relationships, shame, health, etc.)?

Q3. Read John 16:33. What does Jesus say he will give us? What do you think he means by *peace*? How is this peace different from the world's idea of peace?

Q4. Why do you think Jesus reminds his disciples that they will have trouble? In what ways can we overcome life's storms?

Q5. Read Isaiah 42:16. What does this passage mean to you? What are some things God promises that he will do for us during challenging times?

Q6. Psalm 57 says, "The faithfulness of God reaches to the sky ..." That means, it is unlimited! It is unending! It cannot be measured! It will never run out! When was there a time that you witnessed the faithfulness of God? Why is it so important we trust in God's faithfulness?

Q7. How has this chapter helped you?

Read chapter two, "Where Is God?"

Session 3

Q1. Was there ever a time when you questioned God? Explain. In the story, Alex talks about how God answered his mother's prayer through an unexpected visitor. Was there ever a time when God answered you in an unexpected way? Explain.

Q2. Read Mark 4:35–36. What was the first thing Jesus said to his disciples in verse 35? Why do you think Jesus said this to them? Do you think it was important for Jesus to be with the disciples in their boat? Why? In what ways has God been with you during your storms?

Q3. Read Mark 4:37–38. How does Mark describe the storm in verse 37? What was Jesus doing in verse 38? How did the disciples respond to Jesus? In what ways are we like the disciples?

Q4. Read Mark 4:39. How does Jesus respond to the disciples' plea for help? What does Jesus say to the storm? What happened? What does this teach us about Jesus when we face difficult times?

Q5. Read Mark 4:40–41. Why do you think Jesus rebuked his disciples? What did he say to them? What point is Jesus trying to get across to his followers? In verse 41, how did the disciples respond to Jesus' rebuke? In what ways are we like the disciples in this story?

Q6. Read Proverbs 1:23–28. Why do you think people reject God? How does Proverbs 1 warn us about rejecting God? According to verse 26, how does God respond to those who constantly reject him? Do you think this is fair? Why or why not? According to 1 Peter 5:6, what kind of attitude should we have when asking God for help? Why do you think this pleases God?

Q7. What is one point that has helped you from reading this chapter? Why?

Read chapter three, "Why Do Storms Come? Part 1"

Session 4

Q1. What emotions came to you when you read about Steven? Was there ever a time you experienced a tragedy like this? How did you react?

Q2. Why do you think God gets blamed for all the horrible things that happen to us? If God was on trial, convicted of all the bad things in the world, how do you think he would defend himself? What would he say? Do you think it's fair to blame God for every misfortune that happens to us? Why or why not?

Q3. Read John 9:1–2. What was wrong with the man? Why did the disciples think God did this to him? In what ways do we justify misfortune in our lives and others'?

Q4. Read John 9:3. How does Jesus answer his disciples? According to Jesus, what action is God guilty of? What does this passage teach us about God?

Q5. Read Genesis 1:24. What does God call his creation? Why is it important that God blesses all his creation? What kind of world would this have been? Imagine for a moment what the world must have been like before evil entered. What do you see? What do you feel? What do you smell?

Q6. Read Genesis 3:1–17. What lies does the serpent tell Eve? How does Satan twist God's words? According to verse 5, what is the "real sin" that Satan tempts humankind with? Why are our choices so important? Why do you think God gives us free choice? In verse 17, what happens to God's perfect creation because of Adam's sin? In what ways do we see sin corrupting our world today? What is God going to do about it?

Q7. What is something new you learned from reading this chapter?

Read chapter four, "Why Do Storms Come? Part 2"

Session 5

Q1. When was there a time you had to make a serious decision between right and wrong? What did you choose? Why do you think most people choose wrong over right?

Q2. Read Proverbs 14:12. Was there ever a time you chose your way over God's way? Why do you think people choose to ignore God's way? What does Proverbs 14:12 teach us about depending only on ourselves? What are some things in life that "seem right" to us but may lead us into destruction?

Q3. Read Proverbs 3:5–6. According to Proverbs 3, what are some ways that we can start making wise decisions? Why is it so important to trust God's wisdom rather than our own?

Q4. Read Jeremiah 29:11. How does Billy's story demonstrate bad choices? How different do you think Billy's life would have been if he saw God as loving? How do bad choices affect your life? The lives of those around you? Society? According to Jeremiah 29:11, what does God want for our lives?

Q5. Why do you think God doesn't just remove all the evil in the world? What do you think would happen if he did? What would happen to us?

Q6. Read Romans 5:8. How does God restore humanity from evil? According to 2 Chronicles 7:14, how should we respond to God's gift of love?

Q7. In what ways has this chapter help you understand more about God?

Read chapter five, "Preparing for Storms"

Session 6

Q1. Name one event in your life that took a lot of preparation. How long did it take you to prepare for this event? What would have happened if you didn't prepare?

Q2 Read Proverbs 27:12. What kind of person takes precautions against danger? What happens if we just ignore our problems? Why is preparing for danger so important?

Q3 Read Matthew 7:24–25. According to Jesus, how should we prepare our lives against raging storms? Why do you think Jesus takes preparation so seriously? What are some ways we can build our lives upon the rock of Christ Jesus?

Q4. Read Hebrews 3:15. Do you know someone who waited too long to prepare for a disaster? What happened to them? Why do you think it is so important to start making preparations today? What are some ways we can hear God's voice today to help us prepare for tomorrow?

Q5. Why did the farmer wait so long to fix his roof? What does the story of the farmer teach us about not preparing?

Q6. How would you answer this question? "Have I become too worried about God *preventing* my every storm than I am willing to let him *prepare* me for any storm?" What do you think the author is trying to get across?

Q7. Which Scriptures spoke to you while reading this chapter? Why?

Read chapter six, "The Power of God's Word"

Session 7

Q1. Has there ever been a time you witnessed the power of God's word in yours or someone else's life? What is your favorite Scripture? How has this Scripture helped you?

Q2. Read Isaiah 55:11. What does this passage mean to you? Why do you think Isaiah said, "It will not return to me empty?" How powerful is God's word, and in what ways does it accomplish? How does this passage give you encouragement when facing challenging situations?

Q3. Read Proverbs 13:11. What does God teach us about money? How does this passage help protect you from economic storms? Read Philippians 4:12. Why is contentment so important, especially in today's world?

Q4. Read Daniel 1:5–15. Why do you think Daniel chose to not eat the royal meat? What did he choose to eat instead? How does this Scripture teach us to make wiser decisions concerning our health?

Q5. Read John 11:25. How does this passage give us hope? In what ways can this passage give comfort to those who are experiencing grief? Why is it so important to trust in Jesus' resurrection power?

Q6. Read Matthew 6:12. Why is forgiveness important? How does forgiveness help heal broken relationships? What are some ways we can practice forgiveness to others?

Read chapter seven, "During the Storm"

Session 8

Q1. Did you ever go through a difficult time? What happened? How did you make it through?

Q2. Read 2 Kings 6:12–14. Why is Elisha in trouble with the king? What does the king plan to do with Elisha?

Q3. Read 2 Kings 6:15. How does the servant react to the king's army? In what ways are we like Elisha's servant when we face hard times?

Q4. Read 2 Kings 6:16–17. What does Elisha tell his servant? What does Elisha do? What does this passage tell us about the power of prayer? What do Elisha and the servant see? How does this passage demonstrate God's faithfulness?

Q5. Read Proverbs 18:10. How is God described? What are some ways God keeps us safe?

Q6. Read Psalm 40:1. What does this Scripture teach us about patience? What does God promise to do if we "be still"? In what ways does this Scripture help you when you are facing a life storm?

Q7. In what ways do you think God is like the eye of a hurricane?

Read chapter eight, "What Would God Say?"

Session 9

Q1. If you could ask God anything, what would you ask? What do you think he would say to you?

Q2. Which question in Chapter 8 can you relate to? In what ways did God's answer help you?

Q3. Read Hebrews 4:15. In what ways does Jesus relate to us? Does this Scripture give you any comfort? Hope? In what ways?

Q4. Read 1 Corinthians 13:12. What does this passage mean to you? According to this passage, why do we not understand everything we go through in life? How does God steer us through life's storms according to Jeremiah 29:11?

Q5. Read Lamentations 3:22–23. If you could describe God's love in only one word, what would that word be? Why? What does this passage tell us about God's love? In what ways have you experienced God's love in your life?

Q6. Read 1 Corinthians 10:13. What does this passage tell you about God's faithfulness? In what ways does this passage help us during trials in life?

Q7. Read 2 Corinthians 12:9. Has there ever been a time when you witnessed God's power in your life? Why do you think Paul said, "his grace is sufficient for you"? Why do you think it's in our weaknesses that God works mightily? In what ways does this passage encourage you?

Read chapter nine, "The Aftermath"

Session 10

Q1. Describe a time when you helped someone through a difficult moment in life. Did this experience help you grow? How?

Q2. Read Nehemiah 2:17. What happened to Jerusalem? How do you think Nehemiah felt when he looked upon his destroyed home? If you were Nehemiah, what do you think you would have done?

Q3. Read Nehemiah 2:18. What does Nehemiah tell the people? What are some ways God uses people in relief efforts?

Q4. Read Romans 8:37. What does God call you in this passage? What do you think this means? How does this passage help you overcome storms in your own life?

Q5. Read James 1:2. Why does James tell us as we go through trials? How does this passage help you gain a perspective on life's storms? Why do you think perseverance is important when up against challenges?

Q6. Read 2 Corinthians 1:5–6. According to Paul, why do we go through trials? In what ways can we help people who go through similar experiences?

How does this Scripture change your perspective concerning the storms you are or have experienced in life?

Q7. How has this book helped you? What questions has it answered? How has this study changed your perspective concerning the storms of life? Of God?

CPSIA information can be obtained at www.ICGtesting.com
Printed in the USA
LVOW030526021211

257444LV00001B/3/P